Learn to Cook
Fabulous Asian
Homestyle Recipes

This handy guide to homestyle Asian cooking
features over 40 delicious recipes from the kitchens
of China, Indonesia, Japan, Malaysia,
Singapore and Vietnam.

PERIPLUS

Contents

Introduction   3

Basic Asian Ingredients   4

Salads and Snacks   8

Soups   18

Vegetables   22

Noodles   26

Rice   38

Fish and Seafood   49

Poultry and Meat   69

Desserts   94

Complete Recipe Listing   96

MAIL ORDER SOURCES

Finding the ingredients for Asian home cooking has become very simple. Most super-markets carry staples such as soy sauce, fresh ginger and fresh lemongrass. Almost every large metropolitan area has Asian markets serving the local population—just check your local business directory. With the Internet, exotic Asian ingredients and cooking utensils can be easily found online. The following list is a good starting point of online merchants offering a wide variety of goods and services.

http://www.asiafoods.com

http://www.geocities.com/MadisonAvenue/8074/VarorE.html

http://dmoz.org/Shopping/Food/Ethnic_and_Regional/Asian/

http://www.orientalpantry.com/

http://www.zestyfoods.com/

http://asianwok.com/

http://www.orientalfoodexpress.com/

http://www.i-clipse.com/

http://www.ethnicfoodsco.com/ShoppingAndMoreMain.html

http://www.thecmccompany.com/

http://www.ethnicgrocer.com/

Ask anyone what they consider "homestyle" cooking to be and they're likely to say it's food that's just like Mom used to make. And it doesn't matter whether Mom is American, Chinese, Indonesian, Japanese, Malaysian, or Vietnamese. The answer is always the same: homestyle food is familiar, it's nourishing, it's simple and it's economical.

In this book, we've compiled recipes for favorite dishes made by moms in the home kitchens of China, Indonesia, Japan, Malaysia, Singapore and Vietnam. It's an exciting array of flavors and textures that provides an overview of how similar these cooking styles can be, but how quickly and easily they take on their own unique tastes with the addition of a different blend of spices, or coconut milk, or shrimp paste.

Most of the items in the Basic Ingredients list that follows are spices and condiments which, when combined, give these dishes their unique and exotic flavors. And once those ingredients have found their way into your cupboard—the spices in small quantities to maintain freshness, and properly stored in glass jars in a cool, dark place—you'll have everything you need to add those fabulous flavors to your everyday meals.

Many of these recipes involve making a spice paste to blend the flavors. Usually, whole spices such as seeds and peppercorns are first heated to release their aromas and flavors by dry-frying them in a dry, heavy-bottomed frying pan until they become aromatic. They are then ground and combined with the rest of the spice paste ingredients. Flavors are also released from ingredients such as lemongrass, garlic and ginger by bruising them, which means mashing them lightly with the side of a knife blade or cleaver.

Homestyle cooking anywhere depends largely on the quality and freshness of the ingredients you use. Almost all of these recipes lend themselves readily to spontaneous improvisation and creative innovation, leaving the cook plenty of leeway to substitute ingredients according to what's available.

With these simple recipes, you can give yourself and your friends a taste of Asia in your own home kitchen. Who knows what you might try next!

Basic Asian Ingredients

Aromatic ginger, also known as *kencur* or *cekor*, is sometimes mistakenly called lesser galangal. This ginger-like root with a unique, camphor-like flavor should be used sparingly. Wash it and scrape off the skin before using. Dried sliced *kencur* powder can be used as a substitute. Soak dried slices in boiling water for approximately 30 minutes; use $1/2$–1 teaspoon of powder for 1 in ($2^1/_2$ cm) of fresh root.

Bonito flakes are the shavings of dried, smoked and cured bonito fish, sold in fine or coarse flakes in small plastic packs. Fine flakes are used as a garnish, while coarse flakes are used to make bonito fish stock (**dashi**). Store unused portions in an airtight container or plastic bag.

Candlenuts are waxy straw-colored nuts that are ground to add texture and flavor to some dishes. Raw, unsalted macadamia nuts are the best substitute.

Chilies come in many shapes and sizes. The relatively mild large red or green chilies are commonly used, while the tiny **bird's-eye chilies** provide much more heat. **Dried red chilies** are sometimes preferred for the brighter color they give to cooked dishes and for their smoky aroma. **Chili oil**, cooking oil that has been infused with chilies, is also used in some dishes. **Chili paste** is a blend of ground, fresh or dried chilies, salt, vinegar and other flavorings. It is sometimes fermented to enhance its flavor.

Chinese cabbage, sometimes called Napa cabbage, grows in a tight, cylindrical head. The outer leaves are light green with a white midrib, while the inner leaves are creamy yellow.

Coconut milk is made by blending freshly grated coconut meat with water and squeezing the liquid from the mixture. Coconut cream, or **thick coconut milk**, is produced from the first pressing, while thinner milk results from subsequent pressings. Fresh coconut milk is best, but canned or frozen coconut milk is convenient and readily available.

Curry leaves are generally sold fresh, dried or frozen in sprigs consisting of 12–16 small, slightly pointed dull green leaves. There is no substitute for their unique flavor. Use fresh leaves if possible.

Daikon is a variety of large white radish, also known as Japanese or Asian radish. They are milder than small red radishes, more like a white carrot actually. Daikon can be eaten raw in salads, pickled, or used in stir-fries, soups and stews. It has a sweet and zesty flavor with a mild bite.

Dashi powder is used to make *dashi* fish stock and is a basic seasoning in many Japanese recipes including soups and salad dressings. It may be substituted with soup stock powder or bouillon cubes.

Deep-fried shallots are a flavorful garnish used for many Asian dishes. They are available in packages in Asian food shops, but you can easily make them yourself by thinly slicing shallots and frying them in oil until golden brown. It's best to keep them frozen if they are to be stored for very long.

Dried shrimp are a popular seasoning in many Asian dishes. Choose dried shrimps that are pink in color and soak in water to soften before use. Look for brightly colored, plump dried shrimp. Soak for about 5 minutes to soften before using.

Dried shrimp paste, also called *belachan*, is an extremely pungent paste made from fermented shrimp. It is available in jars or firm brown blocks. Unless it is going to be fried as part of a spice paste, it needs to be toasted before cooking. Either wrap it in foil and roast or dry-fry it in a pan, or toast it above a gas flame on the back of a spoon.

Fermented black bean paste is made from salted fermented soy beans and is sold in small bottles as a condiment. Some varieties come with chilies and are quite hot.

Fish sauce, a fermented fish product called *nam pla* in Thai and *nuoc mam* in Vietnamese, is a basic seasoning ingredient used throughout Southeast Asia. It is sold in bottles in most supermarkets.

Five-spice powder is a highly aromatic blend of Sichuan pepper, cinnamon, cloves, fennel and star anise. It is used to season many stir-fried meats, marinades and sauces.

Galangal, which is known as *lengkuas* in Singapore and Malaysia, is a member of the ginger family. This aromatic root, which resembles pink-colored ginger imparts a distinctive flavor to many dishes prepared throughout Southeast Asia. It is available fresh or bottled in brine (often more tender than fresh) in Asian food shops and well-stocked supermarkets. The fresh root can be sliced and frozen for future use. If the root is tough, steam it over boiling water for about 10–15 minutes before chopping and processing it.

Japanese rice is a short-grain variety that is slightly more starchy than Thai or Chinese long-grain rice. It is available at Asian food shops and most supermar-

kets. It may be substituted with any short- or medium-grain rice.

Kaffir lime leaves are dark green leaves shaped like a figure of eight. They add an intense fragrance to dishes and are used whole in soups and curries, or shredded finely and added to salads. Kaffir leaves may be substituted with regular lime leaves, lemon leaves or lime zest.

Lemongrass is an aromatic stalk that gives a delectable lemon flavor and fragrance to any dish. The stems are tough and need cutting into useable lengths with a sharp knife. The tender inner part of the base is ground to a paste, or the whole stem bruised and used to flavor curries and sauces.

Lotus seeds are used in both their fresh and dried forms. The oval seeds have a delicate nutlike flavor. Dried seeds are candied and used in desserts and pastry fillings. They can be purchased canned or in bulk in Asian food shops.

Mirin is a sweet liquid made by mixing and fermenting steamed glutinous rice with *shoju* (a distilled spirit similar to vodka). It adds a lovely glaze to grilled foods and is used to flavor soup stocks, marinades and dressings.

Miso is a fermented paste made from soybeans and/or wheat. **Red miso paste** is red to brown in color, high in protein and tastes more salty than **white miso paste**, which is sweeter and milder than red miso. Miso is used to enhance the flavor of soups, stocks and dressings, and as a grilling baste for meat and fish. Miso loses its flavor and digestive properties if allowed to boil. Refrigerate after opening.

Mitsuba, sometimes called Japanese wild parsley, is a Japanese herb with a flavor that is variously described as similar to chervil, parsley, cilantro, sorrel or celery leaves. The cress-like young seedlings are used in salads, and the stems and leaves are chopped and used to flavor a number of dishes. It is available fresh in the refrigerator section of Japanese food shops.

Noodles come in many varieties, both fresh and dried, and are normally made from rice, wheat or beans. **Bean thread vermicelli** (*tang fen* or *tang hoon*), also called cellophane noodles, are thin translucent threads made from the starch of green mung beans. The dried noodles must be soaked briefly in hot water before using. **Egg noodles** are generally made from wheat and egg and are available in round or flat shapes in a variety of sizes. **Rice vermicelli** are made from rice flour and are dried noodles that can be easily rehydrated by soaking in hot water for a few minutes, then rinsing before further boiling or frying. **Rice stick noodles** are similar to rice vermicelli except that they are flatter and larger, ranging in width from very narrow to about $1/3$ in (8 mm). **Soba noodles** are slender Japanese noodles made from buckwheat.

Nori is a type of seaweed pressed into very thin sheets and baked until dry and crisp. Before use, wave a *nori* sheet over an open flame for a few seconds so that it becomes lightly toasted, or toast it briefly in a toaster oven. **Seaweed flakes** are a flaked form of *nori* sold in small containers. They are sprinkled onto various dishes before serving to add color and flavor.

Palm sugar is made from the sap of palm trees and ranges in color from golden brown to dark brown. It is less sweet than white sugar and has a distinctive, maple syrup-like flavor. If palm sugar is not available, substitute with dark brown sugar, maple sugar or maple syrup.

Pickled ginger is a popular Japanese condiment consisting of thinly sliced young ginger roots pickled in a brine of rice vinegar and sugar. There are two varieties: *shoga*, which is red or salmon pink, and *gari*, which is pale yellow. It adds the crisp flavor of ginger to fish and vegetable dishes and is a tangy addition to stir-fried dishes.

Powdered lime, also called slaked lime or *kapur sirih*, is a paste obtained by grinding sea shells in a little liquid. As an ingredient in batters for fried foods and pastries, it promotes crispiness.

Rice vinegar is used to bring out the natural tastes of foods, almost always in conjunction with a bit of sugar. **Black vinegar** is made from rice, wheat, millet or sorghum, and the better ones are aged. **Red vinegar** is made from rice and is often used as a dipping sauce. Rice vinegars are milder and sweeter than Western varieties, which should be diluted if used. Unless a recipe calls for a specific variety of vinegar, the best choices are rice vinegar or apple cider vinegar; red wine vinegars do not go well with Asian flavors.

Rice wine is used in Asian cooking as a tenderizer and flavoring. A good alternative to rice wine is dry sherry or sake.

Roast pork, also known as Chinese barbecued pork or *char siu*, is cooked very slowly with a sweet glaze, which gives it a distinctive red color.

Sake is a brewed alcoholic beverage also known as Japanese rice wine. Chinese rice wine or dry sherry is a substitute.

Salam leaves are often called Indonesian bay leaves because of their appearance even though their taste is totally different. They are subtly flavored leaves of the cassia family. They are available dried in some Asian food shops. Bay leaves and curry leaves are sometimes suggested as substitutes, but it is probably better to omit them altogether.

Sesame oil is extracted from sesame seeds that have been well toasted, producing a dark, dense, aromatic oil with a nutty, smoky flavor. It is often used in marinades, sauces and soups, or as a table condiment. The most commonly available is Chinese sesame oil. **Japanese sesame oil** is much less concentrated and can be substituted with a mixture of approximately two parts Chinese sesame oil to one part cooking oil.

Shiso leaves are flat green leaves with a flavor similar to spearmint, basil and mint. Fresh basil, or a mix of fresh basil and spearmint are the closest substitutes.

Sichuan pepper, in spite of its name, is not related to true pepper. Also known as flower pepper, or *sansho* in Japanese, this pungent spice is one of the ingredients in five-spice powder. Sichuan peppercorns are available both whole and ground.

Soy sauce, brewed from wheat, salt and soy beans, is available in several forms. The most common is **regular light soy sauce**, a clear medium brown liquid with a salty taste, often used as a table condiment. **Dark soy sauce** (Chinese brands are often labelled "superior soy sauce") is dense black and thicker, less salty and with a malty tang. **Black sweet soy sauce** receives additional richness from extended fermentation and is reduced to concentrate the flavor. A touch of molasses is also added. **Sweet soy sauce** (*kecap manis*) is a very thick sweetened variety found mainly in Indonesia. It is well worth spending a little extra to purchase high-quality soy sauce of any type.

Star anise is a dried brown flower with eight woody petals, each with a shiny seed inside, which has the flavor of cinnamon and aniseed. Use whole and discard before eating.

Tamarind is widely available dried in pulp form. To use, soak the specified quantity of pulp in water for five minutes. Squeeze the pulp with your fingers, then stir and strain the mixture to remove the solids. Discard the solids and use the tamarind juice.

Thai basil is also known as Asian basil. The pungent leaves on purple stems impart a heady and minty flavor and aroma to salads, stir-fries, and especially, to the Vietnamese beef noodle soup, pho. Look for Thai basil at Asian markets.

Tonkatsu sauce is eaten with Japanese-style pork cutlets (*tonkatsu*). It tastes like steak sauce and usually contains tomato ketchup, soy sauce, Worcestershire sauce, mustard and sake. It is available in bottles in Asian foods shops.

Turmeric, when fresh, resembles ginger until its bright yellow interior is exposed. It has an aromatic and spicy fragrance, when fresh. In its dried and ground form, it is a basic ingredient of curry powders. The color of ground turmeric tends to fade if stored too long.

White fungus, also known as dried white wood ears, is crinkly and golden when dry, becoming transparent after soaking. It adds a crunchy texture to dishes and is often used in soups and desserts.

Won ton wrappers are made from wheat flour and egg. They come in various sizes and thicknesses and can be filled with meat, seafood or vegetable mixtures, then steamed, fried or used in soups.

Fresh Shrimp Salad (Vietnam)

A cheery salad with contrasting colors of yellow, green, white and pink, this low-calorie dish is suitable for hot-weather eating. As part of a whole meal, this recipe serves 6, but for a main dish, plan on serving only 2–3 people.

Salad
2 small carrots, peeled and thinly sliced
3 baby cucumbers, peeled and thinly sliced
1 scallion, finely chopped
1 tablespoon chopped fresh mint, plus extra leaves, to garnish
1 tablespoon coarsely chopped cilantro (coriander leaves), plus extra leaves, to garnish
8 oz (225 g) medium cooked shrimp, shelled and deveined
2 tablespoons roasted unsalted peanuts, coarsely chopped

Dressing
1 small red or green chili, thinly sliced
1 tablespoon rice vinegar
2 tablespoons freshly squeezed lime juice
2 tablespoons fish sauce
2 tablespoons oil
2 shallots, peeled and thinly sliced
$1/4$ teaspoon freshly ground black pepper

1 Combine all the Salad ingredients except the chopped peanuts in a large mixing bowl. Set aside.
2 To make the Dressing, combine the Dressing ingredients in a small mixing bowl, stirring well. Pour over the salad and toss well to combine.
3 Transfer the salad to a serving plate. Garnish with the chopped peanuts and reserved mint and cilantro and serve.

Serves 2–3
Preparation time: **25 mins**

Eggplant and Cucumber Pickles (Japan)

2 baby cucumbers cut
  into $^1/_2$-in (1-cm) slices
2 Japanese eggplants
  (about 4 oz/110 g), cut
  into $^1/_2$-in (1-cm) slices
1 teaspoon salt

Serves 4–6
Preparation time: **5 mins**
  + 8 hours standing

1 Combine the baby cucumbers and Japanese eggplants with salt in a medium bowl. Cover with a sheet
of plastic wrap or baking paper and place a heavy
weight on top to press the vegetables down. Let stand in
the refrigerator for about 8 hours.
2 Rinse the vegetables very well under cold water to
remove excess salt before serving. Place a few slices of
each vegetable in small side dishes to serve.

*For best results, use tender young cucumbers and
small Japanese eggplants. Keep unused pickles in the
refrigerator for a maximum of 2–3 days.*
Japanese eggplants *are long and thin and usually
smaller than the Western variety, with sweet and tender
flesh. When sliced, they should be rubbed with a little
bit of salt immediately to prevent discoloring.*

Delicious Crab Omelet (Vietnam)

3 tablespoons oil
1 cup crabmeat, picked clean (about 4 oz/125 g)
2 tablespoons chopped shallots
4 large eggs, beaten lightly
$1/4$ teaspoon freshly ground black pepper
2 teaspoons fish sauce
1 scallion, thinly sliced
1 tablespoon coarsely chopped fresh cilantro (coriander leaves), plus extra leaves, to garnish

1 Heat 1 tablespoon of the oil in a frying pan over medium heat. Add the crabmeat and shallots and stir-fry for 1–2 minutes. Remove from the heat and set aside to cool.

2 Beat the eggs with the black pepper, fish sauce, scallions and chopped cilantro. Add the cooked crab meat mixture and stir to combine.

3 Add the remaining oil to the pan and heat over medium heat. Add the egg mixture and cook until the edges turn light brown. Flip the omelet over to cook the other side and cook until the edges turn light brown, 2–3 minutes. Using a spatula, carefully remove the omelet to a serving dish, garnish with cilantro leaves and serve immediately.

Serves 2
Preparation time: **5 mins**
Cooking time: **6 mins**

Shredded Cabbage Chicken Salad (Vietnam)

Think of this dish as the Vietnamese version of coleslaw, a dish of shredded cabbage with a light dressing. This recipe contains both shredded cabbage and shredded carrots, plus chicken and refreshing mint leaves, turning it into a light yet satisfying meal. You can make the dressing in advance and refrigerate it until ready to use. Serve this dish as part of a larger meal to serve 6: otherwise serve 4.

2 chicken breasts, freshly cooked and shredded (about 2 cups)
4 cups shredded cabbage (about 12 oz/350 g)
1 large carrot, coarsely grated
1 small onion, peeled and thinly sliced
$1/4$ cup (10 g) fresh mint leaves
$1/4$ cup (50 g) roasted unsalted peanuts, coarsely chopped, to garnish
Few sprigs fresh cilantro (coriander leaves), to garnish

Dressing
2 small chilies, freshly chopped
1 tablespoon minced garlic
1 tablespoon sugar
1 tablespoon rice vinegar
3 tablespoons freshly squeezed lime or lemon juice
3 tablespoons fish sauce
3 tablespoons oil
$1/4$ teaspoon freshly ground black pepper

1 Combine the shredded chicken, cabbage, carrot, onion and mint leaves in a large mixing bowl.
2 To make the Dressing, combine all the Dressing ingredients in a bowl and stir to mix well.
3 Pour the Dressing over the salad and toss well to combine. Transfer the salad to a serving plate. Garnish with the chopped peanuts and cilantro and serve.

Serves 4–6
Preparation time: **10 mins**

Won Ton Dumplings with Chili Oil and Sichuan Pepper (China)

8 oz (225 g) ground pork
8 oz (225 g) shrimp, peeled and finely chopped
4 scallions, finely chopped
1 egg
2 tablespoons cornstarch
2 teaspoons soy sauce
1 tablespoon minced or grated ginger
24 fresh or frozen round wonton wrappers
2 red chilies, sliced
2 tablespoons fresh cilantro (coriander leaves), chopped

Sauce
3 teaspoons red chili oil
1 teaspoon sugar
1 teaspoon soy sauce
$1/2$ teaspoon salt
1 teaspoon ground Sichuan pepper

1 Combine the Sauce ingredients in a small bowl, blend well and set aside.

2 To make the dumplings, combine the pork, chopped shrimp, scallions, egg, cornstarch, soy sauce and ginger in a medium bowl and mix well.

3 Arrange several wrappers on a dry work surface and place a tablespoon of filling onto the center of each wrapper. Using a pastry brush, lightly dab some water around half of the edge of the wrapper. Fold the wrapper in half and press the edges to seal. If not cooking immediately, lightly dust the dumplings with flour and place on a rack to dry. They should not touch each other.

4 Bring a large pot of water to the boil. Slip the dumplings into the boiling water and let them boil until they all float to the surface, which means they are cooked. Remove from the water with a slotted spoon and drain.

5 Place the hot dumplings in a serving dish, pour the sauce and stir gently to coat. Alternatively, serve the sauce separately as a dip. Garnish with chili and cilantro and serve immediately.

Serves 4
Preparation time: **30 mins**
Cooking time: **5 mins**

Place a tablespoon of filling onto the center of each wrapper.

Lightly dab water around half the edge, fold wrapper in half and press edges to seal.

Ginger Chicken with Vegetables (Japan)

450 g (1 lb) boneless chicken meat, skinned and cut into bite-sized pieces
2 teaspoons finely grated fresh ginger
$^1/_2$ teaspoon salt
$^1/_2$ teaspoon pepper
2 teaspoons potato starch or cornstarch
1 tablespoon oil
1 medium carrot, thickly sliced and blanched (about 1 cup)
1 small onion, thinly sliced (about 1 cup), soaked in water and drained
Finely sliced *shiso* or basil leaves, to garnish
1 cup grated daikon (about 150 g)

Daikon Dressing
$^1/_4$ teaspoon *dashi* powder dissolved in 60 ml ($^1/_4$ cup) water
2 tablespoons sake
2 tablespoons *mirin*
2 tablespoons soy sauce

1 Stir Daikon Dressing ingredients together in a bowl, mix well and set aside.
2 Drain chicken pieces and stir in grated ginger, salt and pepper. Dust lightly with a little potato starch or cornstarch and shake to remove excess.
3 Heat the oil in a frying pan over medium heat and sauté chicken pieces until golden brown and tender, turning once. Drain on paper towels.
4 Toss chicken pieces, carrots and onions in the prepared Daikon Dressing and serve in 4 shallow bowls. Garnish with onion, sliced *shiso* or basil leaves and grated daikon.

Serves 4
Preparation time: **5 mins**
Cooking time: **10 mins**

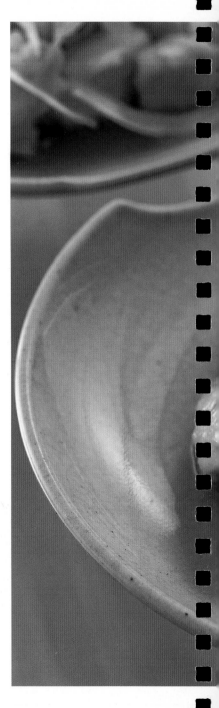

Miso Soup with Clams (Japan)

5 oz (150 g) fresh baby
clams
3 cups (750 ml) water
2 dried *shiitake* or
Chinese black mush-
rooms, sliced
2-inch (5-cm) piece of
dried *konbu*, washed
well
5 tablespoons dark miso
Mitsuba sprigs, to garnish

Serves 4
Preparation time: **10 mins**
Cooking time: **25–30 mins**

1 Soak the clams in cold water for 10 minutes. Drain, rinse well and set aside.

2 Meanwhile, bring a large saucepan of water to the boil. Add the mushrooms and seaweed, reduce the heat to low and simmer covered for 15 minutes. Increase the heat to medium, add the clams and cook covered until the clams open, 2–3 minutes. Discard any clams that do not open. Remove pan from the heat and discard the mushrooms and seaweed.

3 Divide the clams between 4 small dishes using a slotted spoon. Place the miso into a bowl and stir in a little of the hot stock until it is of pouring consistency. Gradually stir the miso mixture into the rest of the hot stock.

4 To serve, pour the hot miso soup over the clams and garnish with sprigs of *mitsuba*.

Spicy Green Papaya Soup (Malaysia)

1 teaspoon shrimp paste, toasted (see page 7)
1–2 fresh red chilies, chopped
4 shallots, chopped
4 cups (1 liter) water
1 small unripe papaya (about ¹/₂ lb/500 g), peeled and cut into bite-sized pieces
1 teaspoon salt
5 oz (150 g) medium fresh shrimp, peeled and deveined

1 Process the shrimp paste, chilies and shallots to a coarse paste using a blender or mortar and pestle.
2 Put the processed mixture and the water into a large pot and bring to the boil. Cover and simmer 10 minutes.
3 Add the papaya slices, return to the boil, cover and simmer until the papaya is just tender, about 10 minutes. Season to taste with the salt.
4 Add the shrimp and simmer until they are just cooked, about 3 minutes. Serve hot with rice.

Serves 4
Preparation time: **20 mins**
Cooking time: **30 mins**

Sichuan Pork Soup (China)

Pork is a very popular meat in Sichuan and this is a favorite way to use pork to prepare soup. The preferred cut for this soup is what the Chinese call *wu hua rou*—literally "five flowered flesh"—which refers to the belly meat, or bacon cut, with its flowery pattern of fat and flesh. Leaner cuts may also be used. This is also a good example of how the famous Sichuan peppercorn can wake up an otherwise sleepy soup with its pungent flavor.

4 cups (1 liter) chicken
  or vegetable stock
  (made from chicken
  or vegetable bouillon
  cubes) or water
4 slices ginger
2 scallions, each cut into
  3 sections
10 Sichuan peppercorns
1 daikon (about 7 oz/
  220 g), halved length-
  wise and sliced
10 oz (300 g) pork belly,
  or other tender cut,
  washed and cut into
  very thin slices

Sauce
2 teaspoons salt
1 teaspoon sugar
$1/_2$ teaspoon freshly
  ground black pepper
2 teaspoons rice wine
2 teaspoons sesame oil

Serves 4
Preparation time: **15 mins**
Cooking time: **20 mins**

1 Mix the Sauce ingredients well and set aside.
2 Bring the chicken or vegetable stock or water to the boil in a pot and add the ginger, scallions and pep-percorns. Add the Sauce and daikon slices and stir. Lower the heat to medium and simmer covered for about 12 minutes.
3 Add the pork, stir, cover again and simmer for 3 more minutes, then turn off the heat completely.
4 Before serving, discard the ginger and scallions. Transfer the soup to a soup bowl to serve at the table, or ladle individual servings into bowls.

This soup may also be prepared with beef or lamb. The best choice from the point of view of health is lamb, because lamb fat is far more digestible and actually benefits the human liver and heart, rather than clogging them up. You may also try using fresh fish fillets cut into thin strips, in which case you should reduce the final cooking time (when the fish is added to the soup) to only 1 minute. Freshly chopped cilantro (coriander leaves) or parsley may be sprinkled onto each individual serving as a garnish.

Spicy Chili Potato Chips (Indonesia)

4 medium potatoes
  (about 2 lbs/1 kg),
  thinly sliced
Oil for deep-frying
2 tablespoons chopped
  celery leaves, to garnish

Spice Paste
2–3 medium red chilies
  (about 2 oz/60 g)
2 shallots
1 teaspoon salt
2 tablespoons oil
2 teaspoons sugar
5 tablespoons lime juice

1 Deep-fry the potatoes until crispy and golden brown. Drain on paper towels and set aside.
2 To make the Spice Paste, blend the chilies, shallots, salt and oil in a blender or food processor until smooth. Transfer to a pan and sauté over low heat until fragrant, about 7 minutes. Add the sugar and lime juice and stir for 1–2 minutes.
3 Add the sliced potatoes to the Spice Paste, stir carefully for about 5 minutes to heat the potatoes and coat them with the Spice Paste. Serve hot, garnished with the celery leaves.

Serves 4
Preparation time: **15 mins**
Cooking time: **20 mins**

Eggplant with Red Sauce (Indonesia)

8–10 Asian eggplants
(about 2 lbs/900 g),
cut in half lengthwise
3 tablespoons oil

Spice Paste
2 tablespoons oil
2 medium shallots sliced
3–4 medium red chilies
(about 2$^1/_2$ oz/75 g)
1 teaspoon salt
1 medium tomato, chopped (about 1$^3/_4$ cups)
1 tablespoon freshly
squeezed lime or
lemon juice
2–3 tablespoons water

1 Heat the oil in a pan and fry the Asian eggplants until golden brown. Drain on paper towels, then set aside. Discard the oil.

2 To make the Spice Paste, blend the oil, shallots, chilies and salt to form a smooth paste. Sauté the paste for 5 minutes, then add the tomatoes and sauté until soft. Add the lime or lemon juice. If the Spice Paste becomes too dry, add a little water.

3 Coat the eggplants generously with the Spice Paste and serve.

Serves 6–8
Preparation time: **10 mins**
Cooking time: **15 mins**

Cabbage with Dried Shrimp (China)

In Chinese, this dish is called *kai yang bai tsai*, which simply means dried shrimp cabbage. It's a very old Sichuan way of cooking cabbage, with the shrimp serving both a culinary role as a counterpoint to the cabbage, as well as a nutritional role by adding vital minerals from the sea to complement the nutrients contained in the cabbage.

$1/_4$ cup (30 g) small dried shrimp
2 tablespoons rice wine
1 head Chinese (Napa) cabbage (about $1^1/_2$ lbs/675 g)
2 tablespoons oil
2 slices ginger, julienned
2 scallions, halved, then cut in strips

Sauce
2 teaspoons sesame oil
$1/_2$ teaspoon ground black pepper
1 teaspoon vinegar
1 teaspoon sugar
1 teaspoon salt

Serves 4
Preparation time: **20 mins**
Cooking time: **20 mins**

1 Place the dried shrimp in a small bowl and cover with the rice wine. Leave to soak for 10–15 minutes, then drain and set aside.

2 Wash and drain the cabbage. Separate the large leaves, cut each leaf in half lengthwise, then cut each half into pieces about 2 in (5 cm) wide. Cut the core into similarly sized pieces. Set both aside to drain.

3 Combine the Sauce ingredients and set aside.

4 Heat the oil in a wok until hot, then add the ginger, scallions and shrimp. Stir-fry until their aromas are released, about 2 minutes.

5 Add the cut cabbage and toss until the leaves are coated with oil. Add the sauce and stir to mix well. Cover the wok, lower the heat to medium and simmer until the cabbage is soft and tender, about 12–15 minutes. Check occasionally to see if the cabbage is done and that it does not get scorched. Remove to a dish and serve hot.

If you are vegetarian, or if you would like to try a different version of this dish, you may replace the dried shrimp with pickled turnips, which add an equally distinctive flavor to the dish as the shrimp, and which also have their own nutritional benefits. Do not try this recipe with the round Western type of cabbage.

Stir-fried Rice Noodles (Japan)

5 oz (150 g) dried rice vermicelli (*mifen*)
2 tablespoons oil
3$^1/_2$ oz (100 g) pork fillet, thinly sliced in bite-sized
  pieces
2 tablespoons grated fresh ginger
1 small carrot, peeled and julienned (about $^2/_3$ cup)
$^1/_4$ cup (50 g) fresh or canned bamboo shoots, boiled,
  rinsed and thinly sliced
3 dried *shiitake* or Chinese mushrooms, soaked in hot
  water for 10 minutes and sliced, soaking liquid
  reserved
1 cup (60 g) beansprouts, rinsed and trimmed
7 garlic chives, sliced into short lengths (optional)
$^1/_3$ cup (80 ml) sake
2 tablespoons *mirin*
1$^1/_2$ teaspoons salt
$^1/_2$ teaspoon ground black pepper

1 Bring a pot of water to the boil and blanch the noodles until just softened, exactly 2 minutes. Drain and cut into shorter lengths using kitchen scissors, then set aside.

2 Heat 2 teaspoons of the oil in a large frying pan or wok over high heat and stir-fry the pork for 2 minutes. Add the grated ginger and continue to cook until fragrant and pork is almost cooked, about 1 minute. Remove from the pan and set aside.

3 Reduce the heat to medium and add the remaining oil. Add the carrots and bamboo shoots and stir-fry for 2 minutes. Add the mushrooms and cook until carrots are tender, about 2 minutes.

4 Return the meat to the pan, then add the cooked noodles, beansprouts and garlic chives. Season with the sake, *mirin*, salt and pepper. Toss until well combined and heated through. Serve immediately.

Serves 2–3
Preparation time: **20 mins**
Cooking time: **20 mins**

Classic Stir-fried Soba Noodles (Japan)

1¹/₄ lbs (550 g) fresh or
13 oz (360 g) dried
soba noodles
2 tablespoons Japanese
sesame oil, or 1 table-
spoon Chinese sesame
oil plus 1 tablespoon
cooking oil
¹/₂ small onion, cut into
thin wedges
1 medium carrot, peeled
and julienned
3¹/₂ oz (100 g) pork
fillet, thinly sliced
1 small bell pepper
(capsicum), thinly sliced
1 teaspoon minced garlic
¹/₂ head Chinese (Napa)
cabbage, shredded
(about 2 cups)
2 tablespoons sake
1 tablespoon soy sauce
5 tablespoons bottled
tonkatsu sauce
4 tablespoons pickled
ginger, to garnish
4 tablespoons dried sea-
weed flakes, to garnish
4 tablespoons dried
bonito flakes, to garnish

1 If using dried noodles, cook according to the pack-
age instructions. Rinse in cold water to remove excess
surface starch, then drain well until dry.
2 Heat the oil in a large frying pan or wok over high
heat. Add the onions and carrots, stir-frying until the
onion is translucent, about 2 minutes. Add pork and
bell peppers and continue stir-frying for another
2 minutes. Add the garlic and cabbage and stir-fry
until the cabbage starts to wilt, about 2 minutes.
3 Add the noodles, sake and soy sauce and stir-fry until
the noodles are heated through. Stir in the tonkatsu
sauce and serve hot, topped with pickled ginger, seaweed flakes and bonito flakes.

Serves 4
Preparation time: **10–12 mins**
Cooking time: **18–20 mins**

Stir-fried Egg Noodles with Beansprouts and Scallions (China)

1 tablespoon olive oil

2 slices ginger, julienned

1 shallot, sliced

2^1/$_2$ cups (200 g) beansprouts, tails trimmed, rinsed and drained

3 cups (750 ml) water

5 oz (150 g) dry egg noodles

2 tablespoons cilantro (coriander leaves), to garnish

3 scallions, chopped, to garnish

Seasoning

2 tablespoons dark soy sauce

1 tablespoon oyster sauce

1 teaspoon sugar

^{1}/$_4$ teaspoon ground white pepper

1 teaspoon sesame oil

1 Heat the oil in a wok or frying pan and sauté the ginger and shallot until fragrant. Toss in the beansprouts and stir-fry for 2 minutes. Remove and set aside.

2 Bring the water to the boil in a large pot. Blanch the noodles in the boiling water until soft, about 1 minute. Rinse in cold water, drain and set aside.

3 Put the Seasoning ingredients into the wok and bring to the boil. Add the beansprouts and noodles, tossing to mix evenly. Garnish with the cilantro and scallions and serve.

Serves 2

Preparation time: **20 mins**

Cooking time: **20 mins**

Sauté the ginger and shallot until fragrant, then toss in the beansprouts.

Blanch noodles for about 1 minute before removing and rinsing in cold water.

Singapore-style Hokkien Noodles

9 oz (250 g) dried thick
egg noodles or 1 lb
(450 g) fresh Hokkien
noodles
5 oz (150 g) dried rice
vermicelli, soaked in
hot water to soften,
drained and cut into
3-in (7^1/$_2$-cm) lengths
2 cups (500 ml) water
8 oz (225 g) pork fillet
3 tablespoons oil
10 oz (300 g) small fresh
shrimp, peeled and
deveined, tails left
intact (heads and
shells reserved)
8–10 cloves garlic,
smashed
2 eggs, lightly beaten
3 cups (240 g) bean-
sprouts, tails trimmed
and rinsed
1 teaspoon salt
^{1}/$_2$ teaspoon ground
white pepper
1 scallion, cut in ^{3}/$_4$-in
(2-cm) lengths
4 small green limes, cut
in half, to garnish

Sambal Belachan
4–6 medium red chilies,
sliced
^{1}/$_4$ teaspoon salt
1 teaspoon dried shrimp
paste, toasted (page 7)

Serves 4–6
Preparation time: **25 mins**
Cooking time: **25 mins**

1 To make the Sambal Belachan, process or pound
the chilies, salt and shrimp paste until finely ground.
2 If using dried egg noodles, put the noodles in a bowl
and cover with boiling water. Let stand for 1 minute,
then drain and add to the rice vermicelli.
3 Boil the water in a small pot, add the pork and boil
over high heat for 10 minutes. Drain, reserving the
stock. Slice the pork into thin strips and set aside.
4 Heat 1 tablespoon of the oil in a saucepan and stir-
fry the reserved shrimp heads and shells until pink.
Add 1 cup (250 ml) of pork stock and bring to the
boil, then cover and simmer for 5 minutes. Strain the
stock, discarding the heads and shells. Return the
stock to the pan, add the shrimp and simmer until
just cooked, about 3 minutes. Strain, then reserve the
stock and shrimp separately. (The recipe can be prepared in advance to this stage and all ingredients
refrigerated for several hours.)
5 Heat the remaining 2 tablespoons of oil in a wok
over medium heat and stir-fry the garlic until it turns
golden brown and flavors the oil. Discard the garlic
and raise the heat. When oil is very hot, pour in the
beaten eggs and stir for 1 minute. Add the noodles,
beansprouts and ^{1}/$_2$ cup (125 ml) of the reserved stock.
Stir-fry over high heat for 1 minute, then add the
pork, shrimp, salt and pepper. Stir-fry until everything is heated through and well mixed, 2–3 minutes,
adding a little more stock if the noodles stick. Add
the scallions and stir-fry for a few seconds more.
6 Transfer the noodles to a large serving dish. Serve
with Sambal Belachan and limes on the side or, if
preferred, small bowls of dark soy sauce with sliced
large red chilies.

*For a variation, substitute fresh squid for half of the
shrimp. Slice cleaned squid into rings and simmer
together with the shrimp.*

Penang-style Fried Rice Stick Noodles (Malaysia)

5 tablespoons oil
1 tablespoon coarsely chopped garlic
8 oz (225 g) fresh medium shrimp, shelled and deveined
1 lb (450 g) fresh flat rice noodles
4 cups (320 g) beansprouts, rinsed and trimmed
³/₄ cup (150 g) garlic chives cut into 2-in (5-cm) lengths
4 eggs
1 teaspoon salt
¹/₄ teaspoon freshly ground black pepper

Chili Paste
8 dried chilies, sliced, soaked and drained
1 teaspoon shrimp paste, crumbled

Sauce
1 tablespoon light soy sauce
1 tablespoon dark soy sauce
1 teaspoon sugar
1 tablespoon water

Serves 4
Preparation time: **20 mins**
Cooking time: **20–30 mins**

1 Combine all the Sauce ingredients and set aside.
2 To make the Chili Paste, process or grind the chilies and shrimp paste, adding a little water if necessary.
3 Heat 3 tablespoons of the oil in a wok over low heat and fry the Chili Paste until well cooked and the oil separates. Set the paste aside and clean the wok.
4 Heat 1 tablespoon oil and fry half the chopped garlic until golden brown. Add half the Chili Paste and shrimp, frying over high heat until the shrimp are seared. Add half the noodles and prepared sauce. Toss over high heat for a few minutes before spreading the noodles out over the wok.
5 Make a well in the center, drizzle in a teaspoon of oil, then crack 2 eggs into it. Stir to scramble the eggs, then combine with the noodles. Add half the bean sprouts and chives, season with the salt and ground pepper. Stir-fry over high heat just long enough to wilt the vegetables but retain their crispness—about 1 minute. Divide between 2 serving plates.
6 Clean pan with paper towels and repeat with the remaining half of the ingredients.

Hanoi Beef Noodle Soup (Vietnam)

This may well be considered Vietnam's national dish. The Vietnamese eat it at any time of the day, but it is especially popular as a breakfast food. What makes this soup so convenient is that you can cook it ahead of time, storing the stock in one container and the remaining ingredients in another. You need only recombine them and reheat before serving.

1 large onion, unpeeled, halved and studded with 8 whole cloves
3 shallots, unpeeled
2 in (5 cm) fresh ginger, unpeeled
12 cups (3 liters) cold water
4 lbs (2 kg) oxtail
2 lbs (1 kg) beef shank
2 pieces star anise
1 stick cinnamon (about $1^1/_2$ in/3 cm)
1 teaspoon whole peppercorns, crushed
1 tablespoon salt
1 lb (450 g) dried stick noodles (about 7 cups soaked)
$^1/_4$ cup (60 ml) fish sauce
1 lb (450 g) beef sirloin or flank steak
2 large onions, peeled and thinly sliced
$4^1/_2$ cups (360 g) beansprouts, rinsed and trimmed
2 limes or lemons, each cut into wedges
4 chilies, sliced 3 tablespoons fresh cilantro (coriander leaves)
2 cups (60 g) fresh Thai basil leaves

1 Char the onion, shallots and ginger on a barbecue or under a grill until fragrant, 2–3 minutes. Place into a large stockpot.

2 Add the water, oxtail, beef shank, star anise, cinnamon, peppercorns and salt to the stockpot. Bring to the boil over medium heat, skim the impurities from the surface and reduce the heat to low. Simmer for 2 hours.

3 Meanwhile, soak the noodles in warm water for 30 minutes. Drain and set aside. Add enough water in a large saucepan to cover the noodles and bring to the boil. Add the noodles, then drain immediately and rinse with cold water and set aside.

4 Remove the and oxtail beef shank from the stock, making sure these are tender. Season the soup with fish sauce and continue to cook over low heat. When the meat is cool enough to handle, slice the beef shank into thin strips. Discard the bones. Slice the sirloin or flank steak into thin strips and set aside.

5 To serve, divide the noodles among 8 large soup bowls and layer the cooked and raw beef on top of the noodles. Place half the onion slices and all of the beansprouts on top of the meat and ladle the hot broth over the ingredients. Garnish each serving with a lime or lemon wedge, several chili slices and a few cilantro and basil leaves. Serve the remaining onions, beansprouts, chilies, lime or lemon wedges, cilantro and basil leaves, and additional fish sauce on the side.

Serves 6–8
Preparation time: 30 mins
Cooking time: 2 hours 20 mins

Sautéed Beef and Onions on Rice (Japan)

3 teaspoons oil
1 medium onion, sliced (about 1 cup/100 g)
8 oz (225 g) beef round steak or shoulder, thinly sliced
1 teaspoon *dashi* powder dissolved in 1 cup (250 ml) water
3 tablespoons soy sauce
4 tablespoons sake
1 tablespoon sugar
4 cups freshly cooked Japanese rice
3 tablespoons pickled ginger
4 eggs, beaten (optional)

1 Heat the oil in a frying pan or wok over high heat and cook onions until translucent, about 1 minute. Add the beef and cook until lightly browned.
2 Add the *dashi* mixture, soy sauce, sake and sugar and stir to combine. Cook until the beef is done and liquid starts to thicken, 3–4 minutes.
3 Fill 4 bowls with cooked rice, divide the beef and onions between the bowls and spoon over a little cooking liquid. Serve topped with pickled ginger and a beaten egg poured over the top of each bowl, if desired.

Serves 4
Preparation time: 5 mins
Cooking time: 5 mins

Yang Chow Fried Rice (China)

4 oz (110 g) shelled small shrimp (about $^1/_3$ cup)
1 teaspoon cornstarch
$^1/_4$ teaspoon pepper
2 tablespoons olive oil
2 eggs, beaten with
  $^1/_2$ teaspoon salt and
  1$^1/_2$ teaspoons oil
3 cups (2 lbs) cooked rice, refrigerated
4 oz (170 g) roast pork or ham, diced (about $^1/_2$ cup)
2 tablespoons light soy sauce
$^1/_2$ teaspoon pepper
1 teaspoon sesame oil
4 scallions, thinly sliced, to garnish

1 Coat the shrimp with 1 teaspoon cornstarch and $^1/_4$ teaspoon pepper.

2 Heat 1 tablespoon of the oil in a wok or frying pan on medium high heat and fry the shrimp. Set aside.

3 In the same pan, heat 1 teaspoon of the oil and scramble the eggs. Push the eggs to one side, pour in remaining oil then stir in the rice and sauté well. Add the roast pork or ham, shrimp, soy sauce, pepper and sesame oil and toss evenly. Garnish with the scallions and serve.

It is important to use cool rice when cooking any fried rice dish. If hot rice is used, the rice will become soggy.

Serves 4
Preparation time: **20 mins**
Cooking time: **10 mins**

Rice Porridge with Shrimp and Beef
(Malaysia)

1 cup (200 g) uncooked rice
10 cups (2$^1/_2$ liters) water
1 cinnamon stick (about 1$^1/_2$ in/3$^1/_2$ cm)
1 whole star anise
4 whole cloves
10 black peppercorns
1$^1/_2$ in (3 cm) fresh ginger, peeled and bruised
6 oz (180 g) lean ground beef
4 oz (110 g) boneless chicken meat, diced
6 oz (170 g) medium fresh shrimp, peeled, deveined and cut into small dice
$^3/_4$ cup (185 ml) coconut milk (optional)
1 teaspoon salt
4 tablespoons deep-fried shallots
1 scallion, chopped

1 Wash the rice thoroughly. Drain and put into a large pan. Add the water and bring to the boil.
2 Add the whole spices, ginger and beef. Partially cover with a lid and simmer gently, stirring several times until rice is very soft and creamy, about 1 hour. If the porridge starts to dry out, add a little hot water.
3 When the rice is soft, remove the cinnamon, star anise and ginger. Add the chicken and shrimp and simmer for 15 minutes.
4 Add the coconut milk, if using, and the salt. Serve hot, garnished with fried shallots and scallions.

The rice should be cooked until the grains are broken and the texture is smooth, soft and creamy.

Serves 4
Preparation time: **15 mins**
Cooking time: **1 hour 15 mins**

Breaded Pork Cutlets with Egg on Rice
(Japan)

$^1/_3$ cup (60 g) all-purpose flour, seasoned with 1 teaspoon each salt and pepper
2 cups (120 g) bread-crumbs
4 pork cutlets (about 5 oz/150 g)
$^1/_3$ cup (80 ml) milk
Oil for deep-frying
1 teaspoon *dashi* powder dissolved in 1 cup (250 ml) water
$^1/_4$ cup (60 ml) soy sauce
3 tablespoons *mirin*
3 tablespoons sugar
2 tablespoons oil
1 small onion, halved and sliced (about 1 cup)
6 medium eggs, lightly beaten
4–6 cups freshly cooked Japanese rice
1 sheet *nori*, toasted and cut into thin strips, to garnish
4 tablespoons pickled ginger, to garnish

Serves 4
Preparation time: **12 mins**
Cooking time: **20 mins**

1 Place the seasoned flour and breadcrumbs on two separate plates. Coat each pork cutlet with flour, then dip in milk and coat in breadcrumbs, pressing lightly to get a good coating.
2 Heat a medium saucepan over medium heat. Add oil and heat to 325°F (160°C), or until bubbles just start to form around the handle of a wooden spoon lowered into the oil. Drain on paper towels and slice each pork cutlet into thick slices, keeping each portion together.
3 Combine *dashi* stock, soy sauce, *mirin* and sugar in a medium saucepan. Bring to the boil, then remove from the heat.
4 Heat the 2 tablespoons oil in a large frying pan over medium heat. Add onions and cook until soft and lightly browned, about 3 minutes. Spread the onion evenly over the base of the frying pan and carefully place the pork slices on top, keeping each portion together.
5 Pour the *dashi* stock over the pork and onion slices and cook for 1 minute. Pour the eggs over a pair of chopsticks and stir lightly to combine with the *dashi* mixture. Cover and cook until egg is set but still a little wet, about 2 minutes.
6 Slide each portion out of the pan onto a bowl of rice and serve topped with thinly sliced toasted *nori* and pickled ginger.

Hainanese Roast Chicken with Rice (Malaysia)

1 whole chicken (about 3 lbs/1$^1/_2$ kg)
1 tablespoon ginger juice (from grated ginger)
1 tablespoon soy sauce
2 teaspoons honey
1 teaspoon salt
$^1/_2$ teaspoon ground white pepper
$^1/_2$ teaspoon five-spice powder
1–2 baby cucumbers, thickly sliced, to garnish
2 sprigs cilantro (coriander leaves), to garnish
Chili sauce, to serve

Rice
2 cups (400 g) uncooked long-grain rice
1$^1/_2$ tablespoons oil
5 slices peeled fresh ginger
2 tablespoons finely chopped garlic
$^1/_2$ teaspoon salt
2$^1/_3$ cups (600 ml) chicken stock (from chicken bouillon cubes)

Soup
1$^1/_2$ cups (375 ml) chicken stock (from chicken bouillon cubes)
2 cups (150 g) watercress or sliced Chinese cabbage
$^1/_2$ teaspoon salt
$^1/_4$ teaspoon pepper

Serves 6
Preparation time: **40 mins**
Cooking time: **1$^1/_2$ hours**

1 Trim off the neck and fat from the chicken, then rinse and pat dry with paper towels. Combine the ginger juice, soy sauce, honey, salt, pepper and five-spice powder, then rub the mixture all over the chicken (inside and out). Set aside for 20–30 minutes. Preheat oven to 400°F (200°C).
2 Place chicken in a roasting pan and roast in the preheated oven for 40–60 minutes (depending on size of the bird). After the first 20 minutes, reduce the heat to 350°F (170°C). Roast until the chicken skin is well browned and crisp. The chicken is done if the juices run clear, not bloody, when the thigh is pierced with a fork. Remove the chicken from the oven and set aside for 15 minutes before cutting into serving portions.
3 While chicken is roasting, cook the Rice. Rinse rice, then drain in a sieve. Heat the oil in a rice cooker pot or heavy-based saucepan. Fry the ginger slices and chopped garlic until golden brown. Add the rice and stir-fry for 3–4 minutes until the grains are well-coated with oil. Add the salt and 2–2$^1/_2$ cups (500–600 ml) of chicken stock (depending on how you like your rice: dry or slightly sticky).
5 Cook the rice in a rice cooker, or in the saucepan uncovered until the liquid level is just below the level of the rice, about 15 minutes, then cover the pan with a tight-fitting lid and cook over very low heat for a further 20 minutes. Fluff the rice up with a fork and remove the pan from the heat.
6 While Rice is cooking, prepare the Soup. Rinse the watercress or cabbage, removing any bruised parts. Pluck the watercress into 2-in (5-cm) lengths or cut the Chinese cabbage into 1-in (2$^1/_2$-cm) slices. Heat the chicken stock in a pot and add the vegetables. Cook 2–3 minutes until just soft. Season with the salt and pepper.
8 Line a serving platter with cucumber slices and arrange the chicken pieces neatly on top. Garnish with cilantro. Drizzle any juices left in the roasting pan over the chicken and serve with separate bowls of hot soup, rice and chili sauce.

Sweet Soy Chicken and Egg Rice Bowl
(Japan)

4 tablespoons soy sauce
3 tablespoons sake
2 tablespoons sugar
3 tablespoons *mirin*
4 teaspoons Japanese
 sesame oil
10 oz (300 g) ground or
 finely chopped chicken
 meat (about $3/4$ cup)
4 eggs
4 cups freshly cooked
 Japanese rice
2 scallions, thinly sliced,
 to garnish

Serves 4
Preparation time: **5 mins**
Cooking time: **20 mins**

1 Combine the soy sauce, sake, sugar and 1 tablespoon of the *mirin* in a small bowl. Set aside.
2 Heat half of the sesame oil in a medium frying pan or wok over medium heat and fry the chicken using a fork to break up the meat. Cook until chicken is just done, about 3 minutes. Season with soy sauce mixture and cook for another 2–3 minutes or until all the cooking liquid has evaporated. Remove from the pan and set aside.
3 Lightly beat the eggs with remaining *mirin* until just combined. Set aside. Heat remaining sesame oil in a frying pan over medium heat, add egg mixture and stir continuously until firm and the consistency of scrambled eggs.
4 Fill four deep bowls with rice and divide scrambled egg mixture between the bowls, placing on top of half of the rice. Spoon cooked chicken mixture on top of the remaining rice. Garnish with the sliced scallions and serve immediately.

Pan-fried Fish Fillets with Soy (Japan)

3 tablespoons soy sauce
2 teaspoons sugar
2 tablespoons *mirin*
2 tablespoons sake
2 teaspoons rice wine vinegar
1 teaspoon *dashi* powder dissolved in ¹/₃ cup (80 ml) water
6 slices peeled ginger, julienned
1 tablespoon oil
1 lb (450 g) cod or other white fish, cut into fillet
3 tablespoons grated daikon, drained
1 scallion, thinly sliced

1 Combine soy sauce, sugar, *mirin*, sake, vinegar, *dashi* stock and ginger in a small bowl.
2 Heat the oil in a large frying pan over medium heat. Add the cod and cook until lightly browned, 2–3 minutes each side.
3 Pour over the soy mixture, cover and cook over medium heat for 2 minutes. Reduce heat to low and continue to cook until the fish is tender and the sauce has thickened, about 3 more minutes.
4 Discard the ginger and serve garnished with the grated daikon and sliced scallion.

Serves 4
Preparation time: **5 mins**
Cooking time: **15-16 mins**

Golden Fish Fillets with Ginger and Scallions (China)

1/2 teaspoon salt

1 teaspoon finely chopped fresh ginger

1 scallion finely chopped

10 oz (300 g) white fish fillets, such as sole, rinsed and patted dry

2 tablespoons flour

1 egg, beaten

2 tablespoons oil

2 cloves garlic, sliced

2 teaspoons rice wine

1/4 cup (60 ml) fish stock (made from fish bouillon cubes) or water

1 tablespoon soy sauce

1 teaspoon sugar

1/4 teaspoon pepper

1 teaspoon vinegar

1 teaspoon sesame oil

1/2 tablespoon finely chopped ginger, to garnish

1 scallion, finely chopped, to garnish

1 fresh red chili, finely chopped, to garnish

1 sprig fresh cilantro (coriander) leaves, to garnish

1 Grind the salt, ginger and scallions in a blender or mortar and pestle until a smooth paste is formed. Make 3 deep slashes in each fillet and stuff the ginger paste into the cuts. Set aside to marinate for 20 minutes.

2 Sift the flour over both sides of the fish fillets, then coat with the beaten egg.

3 Heat the oil in a wok until very hot, then slide in the fish fillets to fry over moderate heat turning once so both sides are golden brown. Push the fish to the side of the wok, reduce the heat and fry the sliced garlic for 1 minute.

4 Sizzle in the rice wine, then the fish stock or water, soy sauce, sugar and pepper, and stir to combine. Slide the fish back into the sauce and continue to cook until the sauce is nearly dry, then stir in the vinegar and sesame oil. Remove to a serving dish and garnish with the ginger, scallions, chili and cilantro before serving.

Serves 2
Preparation time: **30 mins**
Cooking time: **20 mins**

Steamed Salmon Steaks with Sichuan Seasonings (China)

1 medium carrot,
  quartered lengthwise
2 salmon steaks, about
  1 lb (450 g)
2 tablespoons chopped
  fresh cilantro (corian-
  der leaves)

Sauce
2 tablespoons finely
  chopped garlic
2 tablespoons finely
  chopped ginger
3 scallions, finely
  chopped
1 fresh red chili, finely
  chopped
1 tablespoon sesame oil
1 tablespoon cooking oil
1 tablespoon fermented
  black bean paste
$1/2$ teaspoon ground
  Sichuan pepper
1 teaspoon salt
1 teaspoon sugar
1 teaspoon vinegar
1 tablespoon rice wine

Serves 4
Preparation time: **10 mins**
Cooking time: **10 mins**

1 Place the four carrot sticks in a heatproof dish that fits into your steamer. Set the salmon steaks onto the carrot sticks (this allows steam to pass under the steaks).
2 To prepare the Sauce, place the chopped garlic, ginger, scallions and chili into a heat-proof bowl. Heat the sesame oil and cooking oil together in a pan until they are smoking hot, then pour the hot oil onto the chopped seasonings (it will sizzle a bit). Add all the other Sauce ingredients and mix well with a fork or whisk. Pour the sauce over the salmon steaks.
3 Bring the water to the boil in the steamer. Set the dish with the salmon steaks and sauce onto the rack, cover tightly with a lid (place a weight on top to prevent steam from escaping, if necessary) and steam for exactly 8 minutes.
4 Remove the steaming dish with the cooked salmon from the steamer and set it onto a serving dish (do not try to transfer the salmon steaks to a new dish); sprinkle with chopped cilantro and serve immediately.

While this recipe works best with salmon, you may also apply it to other types of meaty, deep-water sea fish, such as tuna, swordfish, marlin and so forth. You may also use fillet cuts of virtually any sort of fresh sea fish. Some cooks like to use a sharp knife to cut the steaks into bite-sized pieces in the steaming dish after they come out of the steamer. This makes it easier for diners to serve themselves from the dish using chopsticks.

Spicy Swordfish Curry (Indonesia)

4 swordfish steaks (about 1$^1/_2$ lbs/675 g) rinsed and dried
3 stems lemongrass, tender inner part of thick end of stem only, very thinly sliced
1 fresh turmeric leaf, finely sliced
$^3/_4$ cup (70 g) fresh or frozen grated coconut
2 tablespoons oil
10 shallots, thinly sliced
4–5 cloves garlic, thinly sliced
4 cups (1 liter) coconut milk
2 tablespoons tamarind pulp soaked in $^1/_4$ cup water (see page 7)
$^1/_2$ cup lemon basil leaves, to garnish

Spice Paste
2 teaspoons black peppercorns
2 teaspoons coriander seeds
1$^1/_2$ teaspoons cumin seeds
1 teaspoon fennel seeds
1 cinnamon stick (about $^3/_4$ in/2 cm)
1 teaspoon chopped fresh ginger
1 teaspoon ground turmeric powder
4–5 shallots, sliced
1–2 large red chilies, sliced
1 tablespoon chopped garlic
1 teaspoon salt

1 To prepare the Spice Paste, dry fry the peppercorns, coriander, cumin and fennel seeds, and cinnamon over low heat, shaking the pan frequently, until the spices are fragrant, 1–2 minutes. Process to a powder in a spice grinder or small blender. Add the ginger, turmeric, shallots, chilies, garlic and salt then process to a smooth paste.
2 Spread the spice paste over the fish steaks and sprinkle with the sliced lemongrass and turmeric leaf and marinate for 15–30 minutes.
3 While the fish is marinating, dry fry the coconut in a wok over low heat, stirring frequently, until browned. Process in a blender or food processor until it becomes an oily paste. Set aside.
4 Heat the oil in a wok or saucepan. Add the shallots and garlic and stir-fry until softened, 1–2 minutes. Add the reserved coconut, coconut milk and tamarind water then bring to the boil, stirring. Add the marinated fish and simmer uncovered until the fish is tender and the sauce has thickened, about 10 minutes. Garnish with basil leaves and serve.

Serves 4
Preparation time: **45 mins**
Cooking time: **25 mins**

Steamed Shrimp with Chili Soy Dip (China)

300 g (10 oz) fresh
  shrimp or prawns,
  washed and trimmed
  but left whole
1 sprig fresh cilantro
  (coriander leaves)

Chili Soy Dip
2 tablespoons olive oil
2 tablespoons julienned
  ginger
1 teaspoon rice wine
$1/4$ cup (60 ml) light soy
  sauce
2 tablespoons dark soy
  sauce
1–2 tablespoons sugar
$1/2$ teaspoon pepper
1 teaspoon sesame oil
1 small red chili, thinly
  sliced
1 scallion, thinly sliced

1 To make the Chili Soy Dip, heat the oil in a saucepan and sauté the ginger until fragrant, then sizzle the rice wine in. Pour in the light and dark sauces, sugar, pepper and sesame oil. When the sauce starts to bubble, add the chili and scallions. Transfer to a small bowl and serve as a dip for the shrimp.

2 Place the shrimp or prawns in a steamer and sit the steamer in a wok half filled with boiling water. Cover tightly and steam over high heat until the shrimp are cooked, 4–5 minutes. Transfer to a serving platter. Garnish with cilantro and serve with the Chili Soy Dip.

Serves 2
Preparation time: **15 mins**
Cooking time: **5 mins**

Shrimp and Egg Patties (China)

1 lb (450 g) fresh shrimp, shelled and deveined
1 teaspoon salt
1 tablespoon cornstarch
1 tablespoon chopped fresh cilantro (coriander leaves)
1 small scallion, chopped
5 eggs
2 tablespoons oil
1 sprig fresh cilantro (coriander leaves), to garnish

Seasoning
$1/2$ teaspoon salt
$1/2$ teaspoon sugar
$1/4$ teaspoon pepper
1 teaspoon cornstarch
1 teaspoon sesame oil

1 To clean the shrimp, rub the salt and cornstarch into the shrimp, then rinse under a running tap until the water runs clear. Pat dry and cut into small pieces.
2 Mix the Seasoning ingredients and add half to the shrimp in a bowl and stir together with the chopped cilantro and scallion.
3 Break the eggs into a mixing bowl and whisk in the remaining Seasoning ingredients. Add the shrimp and stir until evenly mixed.
4 Heat a wok or frying pan, add the oil and shallow fry tablespoons of the omelet mixture until both sides are golden. Remove the patties and keep them warm while cooking the rest of the mixture .
5 Garnish with the extra cilantro and serve with plain rice.

Serves 2–4
Preparation time: **20 mins**
Cooking time: **20 mins**

Succulent Shrimp Satay (Indonesia)

1¹/₂ lbs (675 g) medium fresh shrimp, shelled and deveined, tails intact
1 tablespoon freshly squeezed lime juice
Bamboo skewers, soaked in water

Spice Paste
4 macadamia or candlenuts, dry roasted until golden brown, chopped
4–6 red chilies, sliced
2 kaffir lime leaves, chopped
¹/₂ teaspoon chopped aromatic ginger (*kencur*)
4 shallots, chopped
1 tablespoon garlic, chopped
¹/₂ teaspoon dried shrimp paste, toasted
1 teaspoon chopped palm sugar or brown sugar
¹/₂ teaspoon salt
2 tablespoons oil
¹/₄ cup (60 ml) coconut milk

1 Place the shrimp in a bowl, toss with the lime juice and set aside to marinate.
2 To make the Spice Paste, process the macadamia or candlenuts in a spice grinder or blender until coarsely ground. Add the chilies, lime leaves, aromatic ginger, shallots, garlic, shrimp paste, palm sugar or brown sugar and salt, then process to a smooth paste (add a little of the oil if needed to keep the mixture turning).
3 Heat the oil in a small pan and add the Spice Paste. Cook over low-medium heat, stirring frequently, until the mixture is fragrant, 4–5 minutes. Add the coconut milk and bring to the boil, stirring. Simmer 2 minutes, then transfer to a bowl to cool.
4 When cool, add the Spice Paste to the shrimp and toss to coat well. Marinate at least 30 minutes. Thread 2–3 shrimp onto each bamboo skewer.
5 Barbecue or grill the shrimp for 2–4 minutes. Turn the skewers to brown on all sides. Serve hot.

Serves 4
Preparation time: 25 mins + 30 mins marinating
Cooking time: 15 mins

Garlic Chili Shrimp (China)

1 lb (450 g) fresh shrimp, shelled and deveined
5 dried red chilies
2 tablespoons oil
8 cloves garlic, smashed and skinned
6 slices ginger, cut into fine shreds
3 tablespoons chili sauce (preferably garlic chili sauce)
3 scallions, sliced in 1-in (2^1/$_2$-cm) lengths

Marinade
2 tablespoons rice wine
1 teaspoon sesame oil
1 teaspoon sugar
^{1}/$_2$ teaspoon cornstarch mixed with 1 tablespoon water

Sauce
1 tablespoon rice wine
1 teaspoon soy sauce
1 tablespoon tomato ketchup
1 teaspoon salt

1 Mix the Marinade ingredients in a bowl, then add the shrimp and toss to coat. Set aside to marinate for 20 minutes.
2 Combine all the Sauce ingredients and set aside.
3 Cut the dried chilies lengthwise and scrape away the seeds and membranes.
4 Heat the oil in a wok, then add the chilies and let them scorch.
5 Add the shrimp, garlic and ginger and stir-fry quickly until the shrimp turn pink and the flesh becomes firm, 1–2 minutes.
6 Add the chili sauce and stir to blend, then add the scallions and the Sauce mixture. Cook for another 1–2 minutes, then transfer to a platter and serve.

Serves 4
Preparation time: **20 mins**
Cooking time: **5 mins**

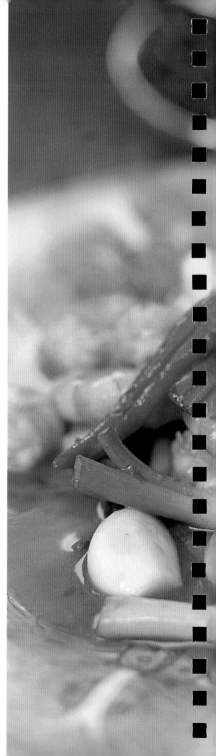

Tangy Sambal Shrimp
(Indonesia)

1 lb (450 g) fresh shrimp
3 tablespoons oil
1 stem lemongrass, thick end only, bruised with a cleaver
$^3/_4$ in (2 cm) galangal, bruised
3 *salam* leaves (optional)
$^1/_4$ teaspoon freshly ground black pepper
$^3/_4$ cup (200 ml) coconut milk
Salt to taste

Spice Paste
4 red chilies (about $3^1/_2$ oz/100 g), seeded
4 shallots
4 cloves garlic
10 candlenuts or macadamia nuts
1 teaspoon dried shrimp paste, toasted and crumbled
3 tablespoons chopped palm sugar or brown sugar
$^1/_3$ cup (80 ml) water

1 This dish may be prepared with shrimp shelled or shells intact (the traditional Indonesian method, as shown). Shell and devein the shrimp, if desired. Trim off the legs with kitchen scissors, then rinse the shrimp and drain in a colander.
2 To make the Spice Paste, slice the chilies and coarsely chop the shallots, garlic and macadamia or candlenuts. Put these in a blender or food processor together with the shrimp paste and palm sugar or brown sugar. Add the water and blend to a fine paste.
3 Heat the oil in a wok and fry the Spice Paste until fragrant and the oil separates. Add the shrimp, lemongrass, galangal, *salam* leaves, ground black pepper, coconut milk and salt to taste.
4 Stir-fry over medium heat until the shrimp are cooked through and sauce thickens, about 15 minutes (10 minutes if using shelled shrimp).

Serves 4
Preparation time: **20 mins**
Cooking time: **15–30 mins**

Black Pepper Crabs (Malaysia)

3 fresh uncooked crabs (about 2 lbs/1 kg)
5 tablespoons oil
2 tablespoons butter
4 shallots, thinly sliced
4 cloves garlic, chopped
1 tablespoon salted soybean paste, mashed
1 tablespoon dried shrimp, roasted and ground
2 tablespoons coarsely ground black pepper
10 curry leaves
5 red or green bird's-eye chilies, chopped
$1/_2$ cup (125 ml) water
2 tablespoons soy sauce
2 tablespoons sugar
1 tablespoon oyster sauce
Few sprigs cilantro (coriander leaves), to garnish

1 Clean the crabs and cut in half, discarding the spongy parts inside the shell. Smash the claws with a cleaver to allow the seasonings to penetrate.
2 Heat the oil in a large pan. Add the crabs and stir-fry for 15 minutes over high heat, or until crabs are half-cooked. Remove, drain and set aside.
3 Heat the pan again, add butter, shallots, garlic, salted soybean paste, dried shrimp, pepper, curry leaves and chilies. Sauté until fragrant. Add a little water if the pan begins to dry up.
4 Return crabs to the pan, then add soy sauce, sugar and oyster sauce. Stir-fry for another 10 minutes on medium high heat. Add a little water if the sauce starts to dry.
5 Garnish with cilantro and serve at room temperature with hot rice.

> ***Salted soybean paste*** *is a richly-flavored seasoning sold in jars. The beans vary from dark brown to light golden in colour and are sometimes labelled "yellow bean sauce". The beans are usually mashed with the back of a spoon before use.*

Serves 4
Preparation time: **20 mins**
Cooking time: **30 mins**

Sautéed Chicken Chunks with Black Bean Sauce (China)

1 lb (450 g) boneless chicken meat, cut into bite-sized chunks
2 tablespoons oil
4 slices ginger, cut into strips
2 shallots, thinly sliced
3 cloves garlic, thinly sliced
2 tablespoons black bean paste
1 red chili, seeded and chopped (optional)
1 green bell pepper (capsicum), cut into wedges
1 red bell pepper, cut into wedges
2 teaspoons rice wine
$1/3$ cup (60 ml) chicken stock (made from chicken bouillon cubes)
1 tablespoon soy sauce
3 teaspoons sugar
1 teaspoon cornstarch dissolved in 1 teaspoon water
2 teaspoons sesame oil
2 scallions, sliced, to garnish

Marinade
2 tablespoons ginger juice (from freshly grated ginger)
2 tablespoons rice wine
2 teaspoons soy sauce
1 teaspoon black bean paste
$1/2$ teaspoon freshly ground black pepper
1 teaspoon cornstarch

1 Mix the Marinade ingredients together. Pour the Marinade over the the chicken chunks, mix well and set aside to marinate for 20 minutes.
2 Heat 1 tablespoon of the oil in a wok, add the chicken pieces and fry over high heat until lightly browned, about 5 minutes. Remove the chicken from the wok and set aside.
3 Lower the heat and add the remaining 1 tablespoon of oil to the wok and sauté the ginger, shallot, garlic and black bean paste until aromatic, 1–2 minutes. Add the chili, if using, and bell peppers, then the chicken chunks and stir-fry rapidly for 2–3 minutes.
4 Pour in the rice wine, followed by the remaining ingredients, except the scallions. Cover and simmer for 5 minutes. Serve garnished with the scallions.

Serves 4
Preparation time: **40 mins**
Cooking time: **10 mins**

Chicken Braised in Sweet Soy (Japan)

4 medium chicken thigh fillets (about 1 1/4 lbs/600 g), with skin
2 teaspoons sake
2 teaspoons soy sauce
2 teaspoons oil
3 tablespoons *mirin*
3 tablespoons soy sauce, extra
3 tablespoons sake, extra
1 tablespoon grated lemon rind, optional
1 scallion, cut into 2-in (5-cm) lengths

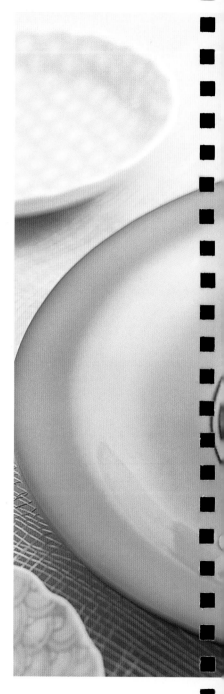

1 Place the chicken fillets, 2 teaspoons of sake and the 2 teaspoons of soy sauce into a medium bowl and marinate the chicken for 30 minutes, or overnight.
2 Drain the chicken and pat dry with paper towels. Combine *mirin*, the 3 tablespoons of soy sauce and the 3 tablespoons of sake in a small bowl.
3 Heat the oil in a medium saucepan over medium heat. Add the chicken, skin side down, and cook until golden brown, 2–3 minutes each side. Add the *mirin* mixture, reduce the heat to low and simmer until the chicken is cooked and glazed and sauce has thickened, another 5–6 minutes.
4 Remove from the heat and slice the chicken into thick pieces. Serve warm or cold, topped with lemon rind and scallions.

Serves 4
Preparation time: **5 mins + 30 mins marinating**
Cooking time: **15 mins**

Fragrant Fried Chicken (Indonesia)

1 fresh chicken (about
2$^1/_2$ lbs/1$^1/_4$ kg), cut
into serving portions
2 *salam* leaves (optional)
1 stem lemongrass,
thick part only, bruised
and cut in 3 pieces
Oil for deep-frying

Spice Paste
5 candlenuts or raw
unsalted macadamia
nuts
1 teaspoon coriander
seeds
$^1/_4$ teaspoon cumin
seeds
2 tablespoons finely
chopped fresh galangal
(about 7 oz/200 g)
2 tablespoons chopped
fresh ginger
1 tablespoon turmeric
powder
2 tablespoons chopped
garlic
1 teaspoon salt

Serves 4
Preparation time: **15 mins**
Cooking time: **35–40 mins**

1 To make the Spice Paste, dry-roast the candlenuts or macadamia nuts, coriander and cumin seeds, then grind them in a spice grinder until fine. Place the ground spices in a blender or food processor. Add the galangal, ginger, turmeric powder, garlic and salt and blend to form a smooth paste, adding a little water if needed to keep the mixture turning.

2 Put the Spice Paste in a heavy saucepan with a tight-fitting lid. Add the chicken and stir to coat with the Spice Paste, then add the *salam* leaves and lemongrass. Cover the pan and simmer slowly over low heat, turning chicken from time to time, until all the moisture has been absorbed and chicken is tender, 30–35 minutes.

3 Heat the oil in a wok until very hot. Add several chicken pieces, with the spices still coating the outside then deep-fry over high heat until golden brown, about 3 minutes. Drain on paper towels and keep warm while frying the remaining chicken pieces.

The chicken can be prepared up to the end of step 2 and kept for several hours or refrigerated overnight before deep-frying.

Grilled Chicken Wings (Japan)

2 tablespoons Japanese
  sesame oil (see page 6)
5 tablespoons sake
12 medium chicken
  wings (about 2 lbs/
  450 g) middle segment
  only, cleaned and
  patted dry
1¹/₂ teaspoons salt
1 teaspoon freshly
  ground black pepper
12 bamboo skewers,
  soaked in water for
  30 minutes
Lemon wedges, to serve
  (optional)

1 Combine the sesame oil, sake and chicken wings in a medium bowl, tossing well to coat. Set aside to marinate for 30 minutes, or refrigerate overnight.
2 When ready to cook, heat a grill or barbecue.
3 Drain the chicken wings. Combine the salt and pepper and rub into the chicken wings. Thread each wing onto a skewer so that the meat is thin and flat and the skewers can be placed to cook side-by-side, as shown.
4 Grill or barbecue over medium heat until cooked through and lightly browned, 10–12 minutes, turning once during cooking.
5 Serve warm with lemon wedges, if desired.

Serves 6
Preparation time: **6 mins + 30 mins marinating**
Cooking time: **10–12 mins**

Grilled Miso Chicken (Japan)

1¹/₂ tablespoons red
  miso
2 tablespoons sake
1 tablespoon *mirin*
2 teaspoons soy sauce
4 large chicken breasts
  (about 1 lb/500 g),
  halved, skin intact
Shredded *shiso* or green
  basil leaves, to garnish
1 lemon, cut into wedges,
  to serve

Serves 4
Preparation time: **5 mins**
  + 1 hour marinating
Cooking time: **8–10 mins**

1 Combine the miso, sake, *mirin* and soy sauce in a
medium bowl. Add the chicken breasts, toss to coat well
and set aside to marinate for 1 hour, or refrigerate
overnight.
2 When ready to cook, heat a grill or barbecue.
Lightly oil the grill tray or barbecue grill and cook,
with the skin side toward the heat, over high heat
until cooked through and lightly browned, 5–8 minutes, turning once during cooking.
3 Cut the chicken into finger-width slices and transfer
to a serving plate. Garnish with sliced *shiso* or basil
leaves and serve with lemon wedges on the side.

Grilled Chicken Malang-style (Indonesia)

1 small spring chicken
(about 1³/₄ lbs/800 g),
quartered
1 teaspoon tamarind
pulp, soaked in 2 table-
spoons water (page 7)
3 tablespoons oil
1 cup (250 ml) thick
coconut milk
1 stem lemongrass,
thick part only, bruised
and cut in 3 pieces

Spice Paste
1 teaspoon black
peppercorns
2 teaspoons coriander
seeds
¹/₂ teaspoon cumin
seeds
4–6 red chilies, sliced
5 shallots, sliced
2 tablespoons chopped
garlic
2 teaspoons finely
chopped aromatic
ginger (kencur)
¹/₂ tablespoon finely
chopped galangal
¹/₂ teaspoon ground
turmeric
¹/₂ teaspoon dried
shrimp paste, toasted
2 kaffir lime leaves,
shredded
1–2 teaspoons finely
chopped palm sugar
1 teaspoon salt

1 Place the chicken in a bowl and work the tamarind juice onto the chicken. Rub well then set aside.
2 To prepare the Spice Paste, dry-fry the peppercorns, coriander seeds and cumin seeds in a small pan until fragrant, 2–3 minutes. Process in a spice grinder until finely ground. Process the remaining Spice Paste ingredients and grind to a smooth paste in a food processor, adding a little of the oil if needed to keep the mixture turning.
3 Heat the oil in a wok and add the Spice Paste. Stir-fry over low to medium heat until fragrant, 4–5 minutes. Add the thick coconut milk and lemongrass and bring to the boil, stirring. Pierce the chicken all over with a fork and then add to the wok. Cook, turning the chicken from time to time, until the sauce has been absorbed and dried to a paste, about 15 minutes.
4 Heat a grill or barbecue. Remove the chicken from the wok, coat well with the sauce on all sides, then grill or barbecue until cooked through and golden brown on both sides, 10–15 minutes.

The chicken can be prepared up to the end of step 3 and kept for several hours or refrigerated overnight before grilling.

Serves 4
Preparation time: **25 mins**
Cooking time: **35–40 mins**

Chili Chicken (China)

Tender chunks of marinated chicken breast are swiftly stir-fried with chili and other seasonings to create this enduringly popular homestyle poultry dish, which may be prepared and cooked in less than twenty minutes. Along with rice and some stir-fried vegetables, this dish may serve as the main course for a simple but delicious meal that appeals equally to adults and children. Adjusting the amount of chili paste easily regulates the "temperature" of the chili taste.

1 lb (450 g) boneless chicken breast, skinned and cut into bite-sized chunks
3–6 red chilies, fresh or dried
3 tablespoons oil
1–2 tablespoons bottled chili paste
3–4 scallions, chopped

Marinade
2 tablespoons rice wine
1 tablespoon soy sauce
$1^1/_2$ tablespoons sugar
1 teaspoon sesame oil
1 teaspoon cornstarch
2 tablespoons finely chopped garlic
2 tablespoons finely chopped ginger

Sauce
2 tablespoons rice wine
1 tablespoon water
1 teaspoon soy sauce
1 teaspoon salt
1 teaspoon sesame oil

Serves 4
Preparation time: **10 mins**
Cooking time: **7 mins**

1 Combine all the Marinade ingredients, mixing well. Place the chicken chunks in a bowl, then pour the Marinade over the chicken, coating the pieces well. Set aside to marinate for 20–30 minutes.

2 While the chicken is marinating, combine the Sauce ingredients in a small bowl and set aside.

3 Cut the chilies lengthwise and scrape away the seeds and white membranes.

4 Heat the oil in a wok over high heat and add the chilies. When chilies are scorched and smoking, add the marinated chicken and quickly stir-fry for 2 minutes. Add the chili paste and cook for another 1 minute.

5 Reduce the heat to low and stir in the Sauce. Cover wok with a lid and simmer for 2–3 minutes. Remove from the heat, stir in the scallions and transfer to a serving dish.

You may add some color and flavor to this dish by adding $1/_2$ cup fresh or frozen green peas, diced carrots and diced red or green bell peppers. These should be added right after the chili paste, but before the sauce. For extra zest, garnish the dish with a generous sprinkling of chopped fresh cilantro.

Spicy Coconut Chicken (Singapore)

2 tablespoons oil
1 fresh chicken (about 3 lbs/1^1/$_2$ kg), cut into serving portions
2^1/$_2$ cups (625 ml) coconut milk
2 stems fresh lemongrass, thick part only, bruised
1 teaspoon salt

Spice Paste
2 teaspoons cumin seeds
1 teaspoon fennel seeds
4 teaspoons coriander seeds
1 cinnamon stick (about ^{3}/$_4$ in/2 cm)
4 candlenuts or macadamia nuts, chopped
6 shallots, chopped
3–4 dried red chilies, sliced, soaked in water to soften
2 teaspoons finely chopped garlic
2 teaspoons grated fresh ginger
^{1}/$_2$ teaspoon turmeric powder
^{1}/$_4$ teaspoon nutmeg powder

1 To prepare the Spice Paste, dry-fry the cumin, fennel and coriander seeds and cinnamon over low heat until fragrant, about 1 minute. Process the spices to a fine powder in a spice grinder or blender. Add the candlenuts or macadamia nuts and process for a few seconds more. Grind the shallots, chilies, garlic, ginger and ground spices to a fine paste adding a little of the oil if necessary to keep the mixture turning. Stir in the turmeric and nutmeg powder.

2 Heat the oil in a wok and add the Spice Paste. Stir-fry over low to medium heat, 4–5 minutes. Add the chicken pieces and stir-fry until they change color and are well coated with the Spice Paste, about 5 minutes.

3 Add the regular coconut milk, lemongrass and salt and bring slowly to the boil, stirring constantly. Simmer gently with the wok uncovered, stirring from time to time, until the chicken is cooked and the sauce has thickened, 30–35 minutes. Transfer to a bowl and serve hot with steamed rice.

Serves 4–6
Preparation time: **15 mins**
Cooking time: **35 mins**

Braised Ribs in Soy (China)

3 cups (750 ml) water
4 slices ginger, bruised
4 shallots, bruised
1 lb (450 g) spare ribs, washed and cut into serving
  portions
1 teaspoon oil
1 tablespoon rice wine
2 tablespoons sugar
3 tablespoons dark rice vinegar
4 tablespoons dark soy sauce
4 tablespoons water
1 scallion, cut into lengths
1 teaspoon sesame oil

1 Bring the water to the boil in a pot, add half the
ginger and shallots and all the spare ribs and blanch
for 2 minutes. Drain, discarding the hot water.
2 Heat the oil in another pot and sauté the remaining
ginger and shallots until fragrant, 1–2 minutes.
3 Add the spare ribs and sizzle in the wine, then add
the sugar, vinegar, soy sauce and 4 tablespoons of
water. Bring to the boil, then reduce heat and simmer
over low heat until tender, about 45 minutes.
4 Garnish with the scallion, drizzle over the sesame
oil and serve.

Serves 2
Preparation time: **15 mins**
Cooking time: **1 hour**

Grilled Pork Ribs (Singapore)

6 cups (1$^1/_2$ liters) water
2 lbs (900 g) meaty pork ribs, cut into serving portions
1$^1/_2$ tablespoons honey
1 tablespoon light soy sauce
1 tablespoon dark soy sauce
1 tablespoon rice wine
1 tablespoon black Chinese vinegar
1 tablespoon sugar
1 teaspoon five-spice powder
1 teaspoon salt
1 teaspoon sesame oil
2 cups (500 ml) chicken stock (made from chicken bouillon cubes)
1 teaspoon toasted sesame seeds, to garnish
1 medium carrot, grated, to garnish
Lettuce leaves, to serve
Bottled chili sauce

1 Bring the water to the boil. Blanch the ribs for 5 minutes, then drain, discarding the water.
2 Put the ribs in a bowl and sprinkle them with the honey, light and dark soy sauces, rice wine, vinegar, sugar, five-spice powder, salt and sesame oil. Stir carefully with a wooden spoon to mix thoroughly and set aside to marinate for 30 minutes.
3 When ready to cook, transfer the ribs and the marinade to a wok or wide saucepan and add the chicken stock. Bring to the boil, cover and simmer for 15 minutes, stirring several times. Transfer the ribs to a bowl. Bring the cooking liquid back to the boil and cook over very high heat, uncovered, until the mixture reduces and becomes thick and syrupy, about 15 minutes.
4 Pour the mixture over the pork ribs and stir with a wooden spoon for about 1 minute to coat the ribs thoroughly with the mixture. Drain the ribs in a colander.
5 Heat a grill, then arrange the ribs on a rack set in an oven tray and grill under high heat for 8–10 minutes on each side.
6 Sprinkle with sesame seeds and serve the ribs hot on a bed of lettuce and grated carrots with chili sauce on the side.

Serves 4
Preparation time: **10 mins + 30 mins marinating**
Cooking time: **2 hours**

Teochew Spiced Duck (Singapore)

1 fresh or frozen duck (about 5 lbs/2$^1/_2$ kg)
2 teaspoons five-spice powder
$^1/_2$ teaspoon salt
$^1/_4$ cup (60 ml) dark soy sauce
2 tablespoons light soy sauce
2 tablespoons sugar
3 cups (750 ml) water
4 cloves garlic, skin left on, lightly bruised
1 cinnamon stick (about 1$^1/_4$ in/3 cm)
5 thin slices galangal or ginger

Dipping Sauce
4 tablespoons black Chinese vinegar
1 tablespoon water
1 tablespoon finely chopped garlic

Serves 4–6
Preparation time: **15 mins** + **2 hours marinating**
Cooking time: **2 hours**

1 Remove the fatty deposits from inside the cavity of the duck and trim away any loose skin. Wash, drain and pat the duck dry with paper towels.
2 Combine the five-spice powder, salt and both soy sauces. Rub the duck inside and out with this mixture then set aside to marinate for 2 hours, turning occasionally, rubbing again and spooning over the marinade.
3 Put the sugar in a wok with 2 tablespoons of the water and cook until it begins to caramelize and turns golden brown. Quickly add the remaining water, garlic, cinnamon and the marinade from the duck. Put the galangal or ginger slices inside the duck and put the duck into the wok. Bring to the boil, cover and simmer until the duck is tender, 1$^1/_2$–2 hours, turning the duck from time to time to ensure it cooks evenly.
4 While the duck is cooking, combine all Dipping Sauce ingredients and divide between 4 small sauce bowls.
5 When duck is cooked, cut into serving portions and arrange on a large dish. Pour over some of the cooking liquid and serve with the Dipping Sauce.

Malay Lamb Curry (Malaysia)

8–10 shallots, sliced
1 tablespoon chopped garlic
4 teaspoons chopped ginger
6 dried chilies, cut in lengths, soaked in hot water 10 minutes to soften, drained
3 tablespoons oil
1¹/₂ lbs (675 g) lean lamb meat, sliced into bite-sized pieces
1¹/₂ cups (375 ml) water
1 teaspoon salt
¹/₂ cup (125 ml) coconut milk
1 tablespoon tamarind pulp in ¹/₄ cup water (see page 7)

Spice Paste
4 teaspoons coriander seeds
2 teaspoons cumin seeds
1 teaspoon fennel seeds
1 stick cinnamon (about ³/₄ in/2 cm)
4 whole cloves
¹/₄ teaspoon black peppercorns
¹/₄ teaspoon ground nutmeg
¹/₄ teaspoon ground turmeric
1¹/₂ tablespoons water

1 To prepare the Spice Paste, dry-fry the coriander, cumin and fennel seeds, cinnamon, cloves and peppercorns over low heat until fragrant, about 2 minutes. Process the spices to a fine powder in a blender or spice grinder, then transfer to a small bowl, add the nutmeg and turmeric and stir in the water to make a stiff paste.

2 Process the shallots, garlic, ginger and chilies in a blender or food processor until fine, adding a little of the oil if necessary to keep the mixture turning. Heat the oil in a wok, then stir-fry the shallot mixture over low to medium heat for about 4 minutes.

3 Add the Spice Paste and stir-fry for 3 minutes. Add the lamb and stir-fry until it changes color and is covered with the spices, about 4 minutes. Add the water and salt, cover the wok and simmer until the meat is tender, about 45–60 minutes.

4 Add the coconut milk and tamarind juice and simmer gently, uncovered, until the sauce has thickened and meat is very tender, about 15 minutes. Serve hot with white rice or crusty bread.

Serves 4–6
Preparation time: **20 mins**
Cooking time: **1 hour 15 mins**

Javanese-style Braised Beef (Indonesia)

1 1/2 tablespoons oil
1 lb (450 g) beef steak,
  cut into bite-sized
  pieces
1 stick cinnamon (about
  1 1/4 in/3cm)
1/4 teaspoon ground
  nutmeg
2 whole cloves
1 medium ripe tomato,
  chopped
3 tablespoons sweet
  black soy sauce
2–3 cups (500–750 ml)
  hot water
1/2 teaspoon salt
1 tablespoon deep-fried
  shallots, to garnish

Spice Paste
1 teaspoon coriander
  seeds
1 teaspoon black
  peppercorns
3 candlenuts or
  macadamia nuts
1 tablespoon chopped
  garlic
6 shallots, sliced
1 teaspoon chopped
  fresh ginger

Serves 4
Preparation time: **15 mins**
Cooking time: **1 1/2 hours**

1 To prepare the Spice Paste, dry-fry the coriander seeds, peppercorns and candlenuts or macadamia nuts over low heat until fragrant and the nuts are golden. Process in a blender or spice grinder until finely ground. Process the garlic, shallots and ginger with the ground spices to a smooth paste in a blender or food processor.
2 Heat the oil in a wok. Add the Spice Paste and cook over low heat, stirring frequently, until fragrant, about 2 minutes.
3 Add the beef, cinnamon, nutmeg and cloves and stir-fry until the meat changes color and is well coated with the spices, about 5 minutes. Scrape the bottom of the pan firmly to remove any dried pieces, then add the tomato, sweet soy sauce and just enough water to cover the meat. Bring to the boil, cover and simmer until the beef is tender, about 1 1/4 hours. Put in a serving bowl and garnish with deep-fried shallots.

You could add 2 oz (60 g) transparent bean-thread noodles, soaked in hot water to soften and cut into 4-in (10-cm) lengths, 5 minutes before the end of cooking time. Alternatively, add 1–2 cubed potatoes about 15 minutes before the end of cooking. For a vegetarian version of this recipe, replace the beef with 1 lb (450 g) firm tofu, deep-fried then cut in bite-sized pieces and cooked for only 10 minutes in step 3.

Chinese Beef Steak (Singapore)

1¹/₂ lbs (675 g) beef
  steak, sliced into bite-
  sized pieces
1 tablespoon cornstarch
1 teaspoon baking soda
4 tablespoons oil
1 tablespoon light soy
  sauce
1 tablespoon steak sauce
1 teaspoon rice wine
¹/₂ teaspoon sesame oil
1 egg
1 teaspoon finely
  chopped garlic
Steamed asparagus or
  broccoli, to serve

Sauce
³/₄ cup (185 ml) water
1 tablespoon
  Worcestershire sauce
1 tablespoon tomato
  ketchup
1 teaspoon oyster sauce
1 teaspoon sugar
¹/₂ teaspoon salt

1 Put the meat into a bowl and sprinkle with cornstarch, then sift over the baking soda and stir with a
wooden spoon to coat. Add 2 tablespoons of the oil,
soy sauce, steak sauce, rice wine, sesame oil and egg
then mix well. Refrigerate the meat in a covered
container, stirring occasionally, for 4–8 hours.
2 Combine the Sauce ingredients in a small bowl,
stirring to dissolve sugar and salt, then set aside.
3 When ready to cook, drain the meat and discard the
marinade.
4 Heat the remaining oil in a wok, add garlic and
cook until golden brown. Raise the heat, add the
meat and stir-fry until the meat changes color, about
3 minutes. Add the Sauce, cover the wok and simmer
gently until the meat is well cooked and the gravy
reduced to a thick sauce, 3–5 minutes.
5 Place the meat and sauce on a serving plate with the
steamed asparagus or broccoli and serve immediately.

Serves 4
Preparation time: **15 mins + 4–8 hours marinating**
Cooking time: **10 mins**

Deep-fried Banana Fritters (Singapore)

1 cup (125 g) plain flour
$^1/_2$ cup (80 g) rice flour
2 teaspoons baking
  powder
$^1/_4$ teaspoon salt
1 cup (250 ml) cold
  water
Oil for deep-frying
4 large or 8 small firm
  ripe bananas, peeled
  (and cut into sections if
  using large bananas)

1 Sift both types of flour, baking powder and salt into a bowl. Gradually stir in the water to make a thick batter.

2 Heat the oil in a wok. Dip the bananas into the batter, turning to coat thoroughly. When oil is very hot, add the bananas and fry until golden brown all over, about 4 minutes. Drain thoroughly and serve warm.

Serves 4
Preparation time: **10 mins**
Cooking time: **10 mins**

Chilled Lotus Seeds in Syrup (Singapore)

$^1/_2$ oz (20 g) white
  fungus
4 cups (1 liter) water
$2^1/_2$ oz (70 g) dried
  shelled lotus seeds
8 oz (125 g) rock sugar
2 tablespoons white sugar,
  adding extra to taste
Crushed ice or 8–12 ice
  cubes
1 cup canned longans,
  drained (optional)

Serves 4–6
Preparation time: **25 mins**
Cooking time: **45 mins**

1 Put the fungus in a bowl and add hot water to cover. Soak for 15 minutes, then cut away any hard or discolored portions and cut the rest into bite-sized pieces.
2 Split open the lotus seeds and flick out any dark bitter core with the point of a knife. Add the lotus seeds, rock sugar and white sugar to the pan and bring to the boil, stirring to dissolve the sugar.
3 Put the soaked fungus, lotus seeds, rock sugar and white sugar in a saucepan with the water. Cover and simmer gently until the lotus seeds and fungus are soft, about 1 hour. Add more sugar if desired, as the ice will dilute the syrup. Transfer to a bowl and when cool, refrigerate until required.
4 To serve, spoon the syrup, fungus and lotus seeds into 4 soup bowls. Add ice and longans, if desired, then serve with soup spoons.

Complete Recipe Listing

Salads and Snacks

Delicious Crab Omelet
(Vietnam) 11
Eggplant and Cucumber
Pickles (Japan) 10
Fresh Shrimp Salad
(Vietnam) 8
Ginger Chicken with
Vegetables (Japan) 16
Shredded Cabbage
Chicken Salad
(Vietnam) 13
Won Ton Dumplings with
Chili Oil and Sichuan
Pepper (China) 14

Soups

Miso Soup with Clams
(Japan) 18
Sichuan Pork Soup
(China) 21
Spicy Green Papaya Soup
(Malaysia) 19

Vegetables

Cabbage with Dried
Shrimp (China) 25
Eggplant with Red Sauce
(Indonesia) 23
Spicy Chili Potato Chips
(Indonesia) 22

Noodles

Classic Stir-fried Soba
Noodles (Japan) 28
Hanoi Beef Noodle Soup
(Vietnam) 36
Penang-style Fried
Rice Stick Noodles
(Malaysia) 34
Singapore-style Hokkien
Noodles (Singapore) 33
Stir-fried Egg Noodles
with Beansprouts and
Scallions (China) 31

Stir-fried Rice Noodles
(Japan) 26

Rice

Breaded Pork Cutlets
with Egg on Rice
(Japan) 42
Hainanese Roast
Chicken with Rice
(Malaysia) 45
Sautéed Beef and Onions
on Rice (Japan) 38
Rice Porridge with
Shrimp Porridge
(Malaysia) 40
Sweet Soy Chicken and
Egg Rice Bowl
(Japan) 46
Yang Chow Fried Rice
(China) 39

Fish and Seafood

Black Pepper Crabs
(Malaysia) 66
Garlic Chili Shrimp
(China) 62
Golden Fish Fillets with
Ginger and Scallions
(China) 50
Pan-fried Fish Fillets with
Soy (Japan) 49
Shrimp and Egg Patties
(China) 59
Spicy Swordfish Curry
(Indonesia) 54
Steamed Salmon Steaks
with Sichuan Seasonings
(China) 52
Steamed Shrimp with
Chili Soy Dip
(China) 57
Succulent Shrimp Satay
(Indonesia) 60
Tangy Shrimp Sambal
(Indonesia) 65

Poultry and Meat

Black Pepper Crabs
(Malaysia) 67
Braised Ribs in Soy
(China) 82
Chicken Braised in Sweet
Soy (Japan) 70
Chili Chicken
(China) 78
Chinese Beef Steak
(Singapore) 92
Fragrant Fried Chicken
(Indonesia) 72
Grilled Chicken Malang-
style (Indonesia) 77
Grilled Chicken Wings
(Japan) 74
Grilled Pork Ribs
(Singapore) 84
Javanese-style Braised
Beef (Indonesia) 91
Malay Lamb Curry
(Malaysia) 88
Miso Chicken
(Japan) 75
Sautéed Chicken Chunks
with Black Bean Sauce
(China) 69
Spicy Coconut Chicken
(Singapore) 81
Teochew Spiced Duck
(Singapore) 86

Desserts

Chilled Lotus Seeds In
Syrup (Singapore) 95
Deep-fried Banana
Fritters (Singapore) 94